SAM
The Garbage Hound

BY CHARNAN SIMON

ILLUSTRATED BY GARY BIALKE

Rookie reader®

CHILDREN'S PRESS®
A Division of Grolier Publishing
New York London Hong Kong Sydney
Danbury, Connecticut

For the real Sam and all his friends:
Emma, Dasher, Sadie, Mocha, Addie, Rocky, Belle, Sophie, Annie, Lungi,
Gretchen, Bear, Scout, Cooper, Toby, Dusty, Mollie, Cookie, Rags, Josh, Pal,
and the rest of the dogs in the woods

— C. S.

To Auggie, Wiley, and Barkley

— G. B.

Library of Congress Cataloging–in–Publication–Data

Simon, Charnan.
Sam the garbage hound / by Charnan Simon; illustrations by Gary Bialke.
p. cm. — (A rookie reader)
Summary: Sam, a lonely garbage hound who lives at the dump, goes home
with Rosie and her mother and discovers the joys of a loving home.
ISBN 0-516-02057-9 (lib. bdg.) — ISBN 0-516-26078-2 (pbk.)
[1. Dogs—Fiction.] I. Bialke, Gary, ill. II. Title. III. Series.

PZ7.S6035Sam 1996   96-2085
[E]—dc20   CIP
                                                  AC

Sam was a garbage hound.

CAUTION:
DO NOT
PLAY ON
OR AROUND

JUNK

He lived at the dump.

He ate canned food.

6

He slept in a snug bed.

He chased flies for fun.

11

It was a good life,

but Sam was lonely.

15

One day Rosie and her mother
came to the dump.

When they left,
Sam went with them.

19

Now Sam lives in a house.

He still eats canned food.

He still sleeps in a snug bed.

And he still chases flies for fun.

Sam is not lonely anymore.

But he will always be
a garbage hound.

ABOUT THE AUTHOR

Charnan Simon lives in Madison, Wisconsin, with her husband, Tom Kazunas, her daughters, Ariel and Hana, and the real Sam, who is part collie and part golden retriever. This Sam makes up for his lack of taste and manners by his sunny disposition, affectionate nature, and boundless energy.

Charnan used to be an editor at *Cricket* magazine and sometimes works at a children's bookstore called Pooh Corner. She spends much of her time reading and writing books, enjoying her family, and buying shoes to replace the ones Sam eats for breakfast!

ABOUT THE ILLUSTRATOR

Born in the Midwest and trained as an illustrator while still a pup, Gary Bialke journeyed to the soggy environs of the Pacific Northwest to pursue an animation career. After ten years of creative bliss in this field, his job was replaced by a computer.

Gary now resides in Portland, Oregon, with three large dogs and a vacuum cleaner. He hopes to one day find enough success as an artist to give up his paper route.